Fill in the numbers on the clock.

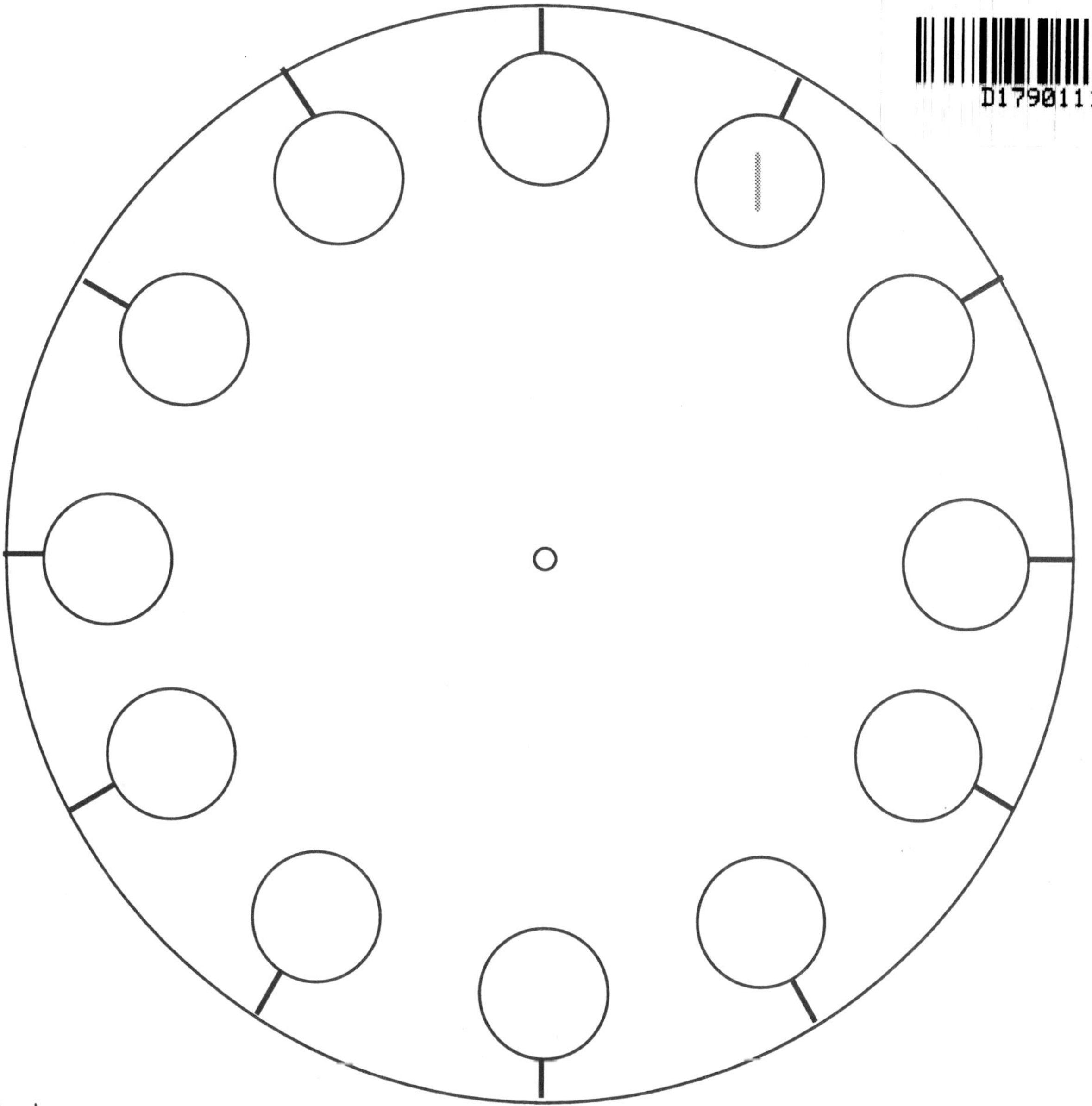

Match the part to its name.

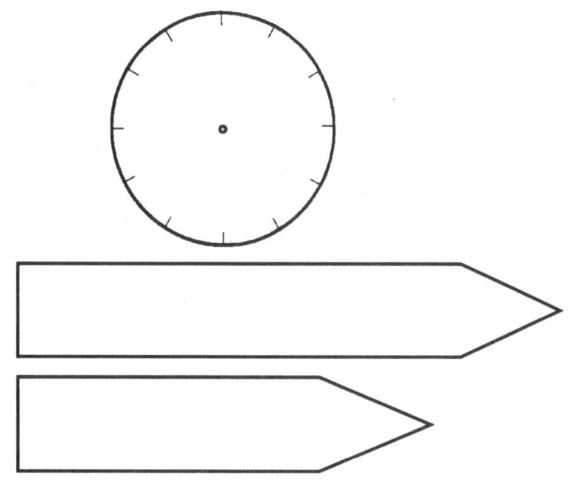

- hour hand

- minute hand

- face

What is the hour?

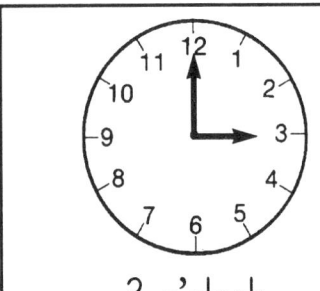 

3 o'clock   5 o'clock   8:00

Circle.

 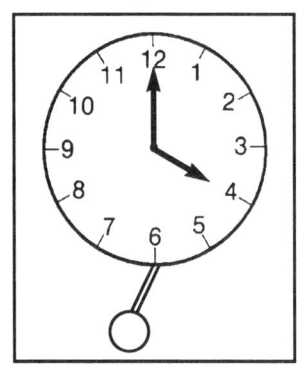 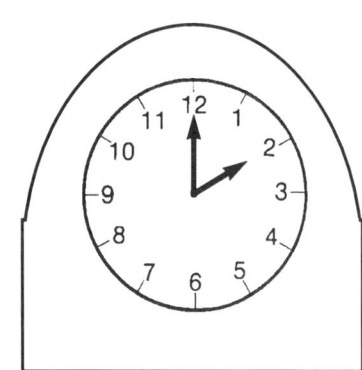

2 o'clock   4 o'clock   6 o'clock
4 o'clock   12 o'clock   2 o'clock
7 o'clock   5 o'clock   12 o'clock

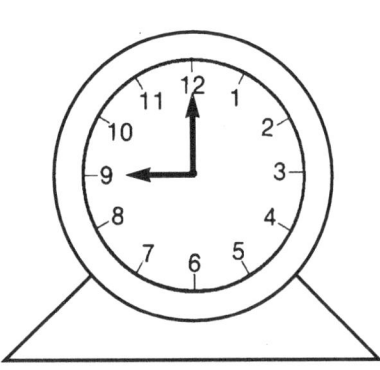 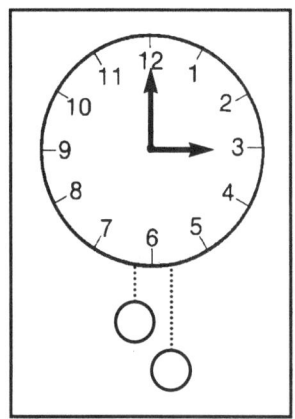 

8:00   3:00   1:00
7:00   6:00   12:00
9:00   4:00   11:00

Match

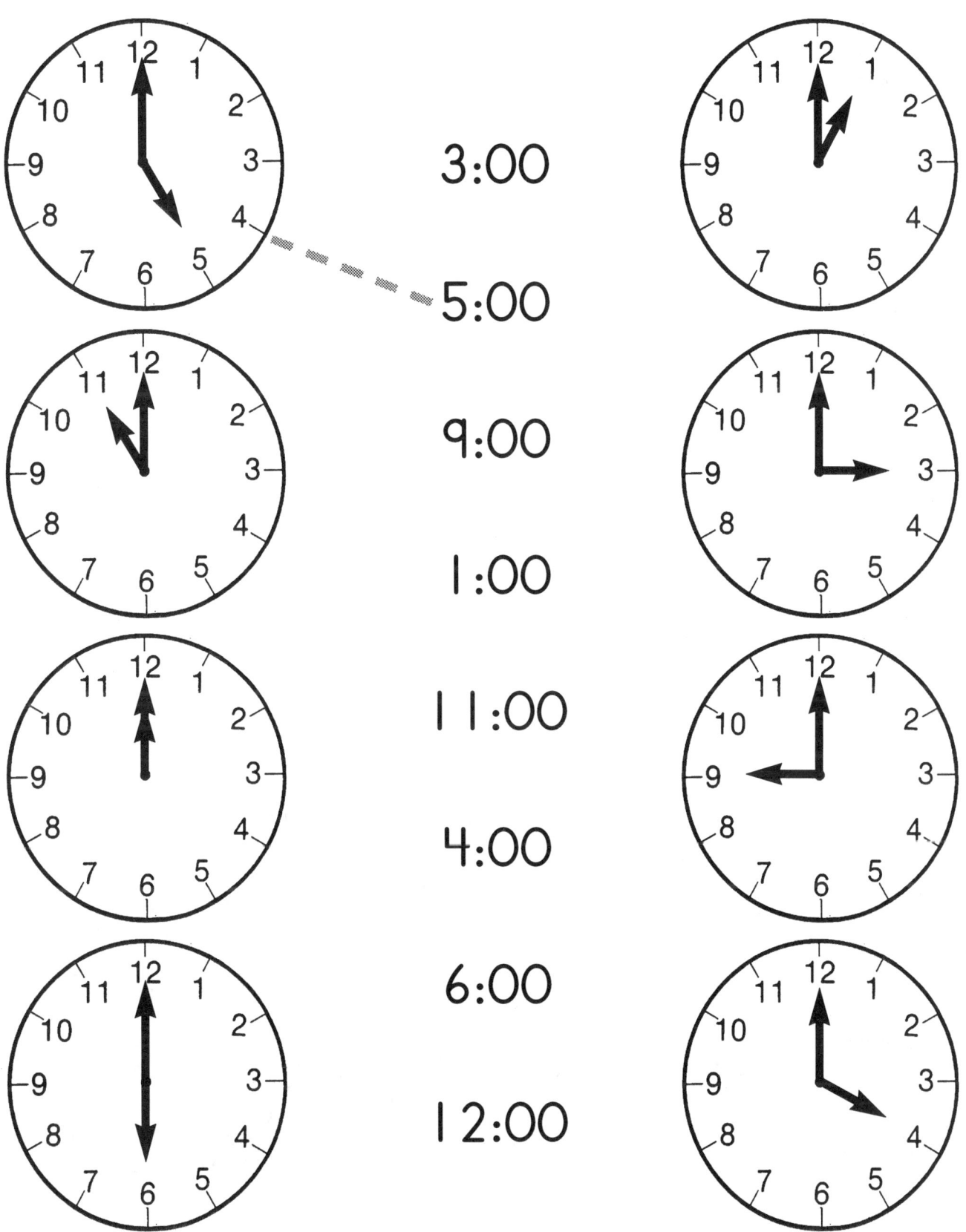

What time is it?

Write the time.

8 : 00

___ : 00

___ : 00

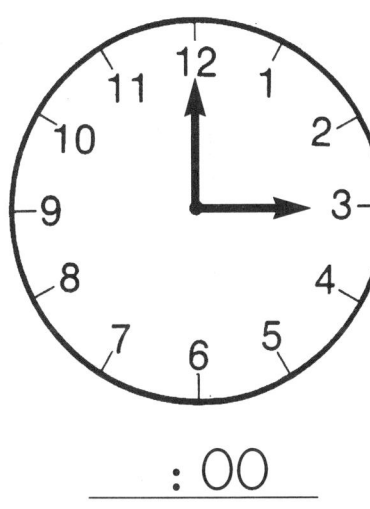
___ : 00

___ : 00

___ : 00

___ : 00

___ : 00

___ : 00

What time will it be in one hour?

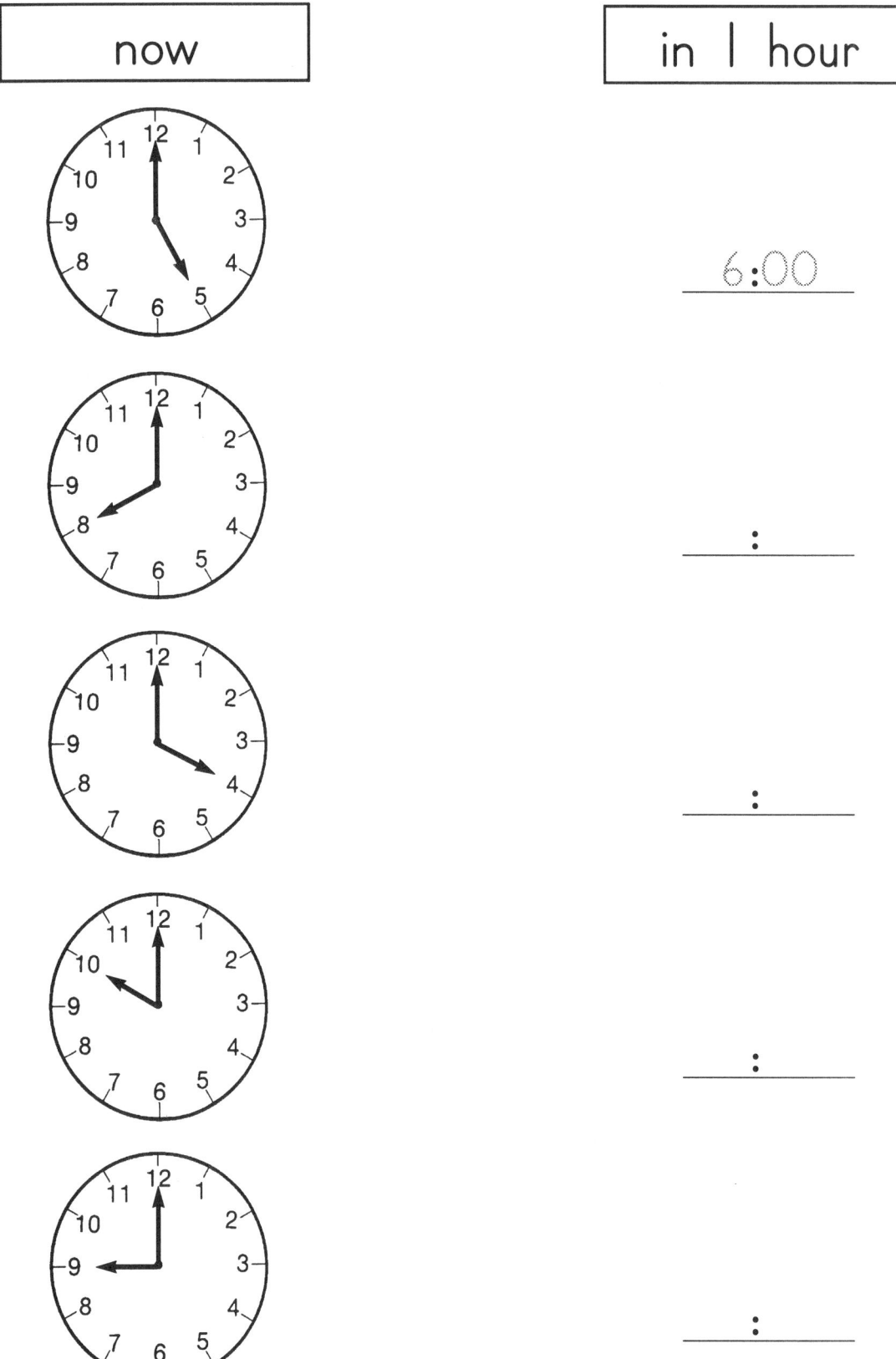

At the Zoo

1. Bob went to the zoo at 2:00.
   He went home at 3:00.
   He was at the zoo _____ hour.

2. Jill went to the zoo at 3:00.
   She can stay 3 hours.
   She must go home at _____ o'clock.

3. Carlos was at the zoo 2 hours.
   He came at 10:00.
   He went home at _____ o'clock.

4. Ann left home at 8:00.
   It took 1 hour to get to the zoo.
   She got to the zoo at _____ o'clock.

Half Past the Hour

2:30
half past 2

8:30
half past 8

Match.

4:30

9:30

5:30

1:30

7:30

11:30

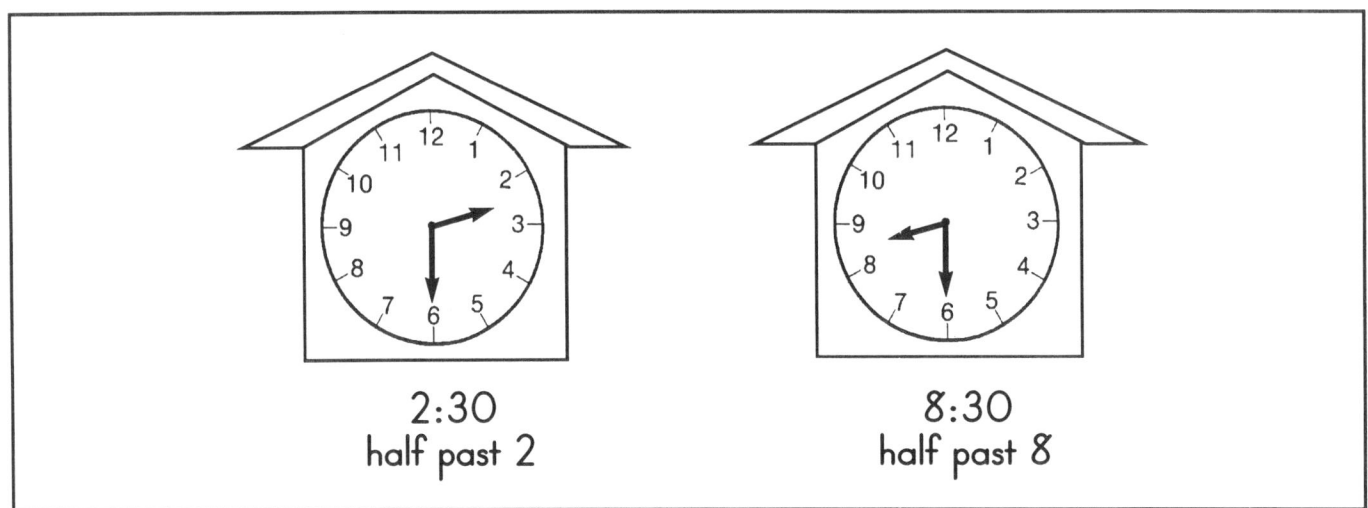

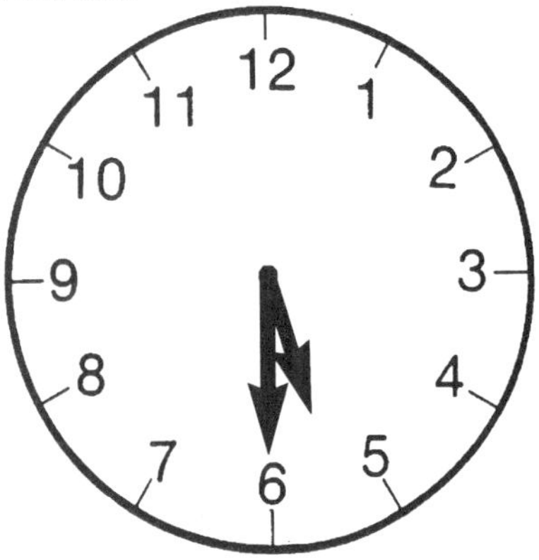

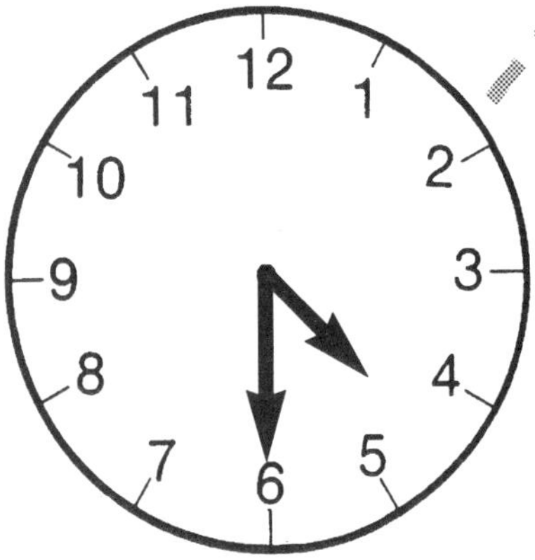

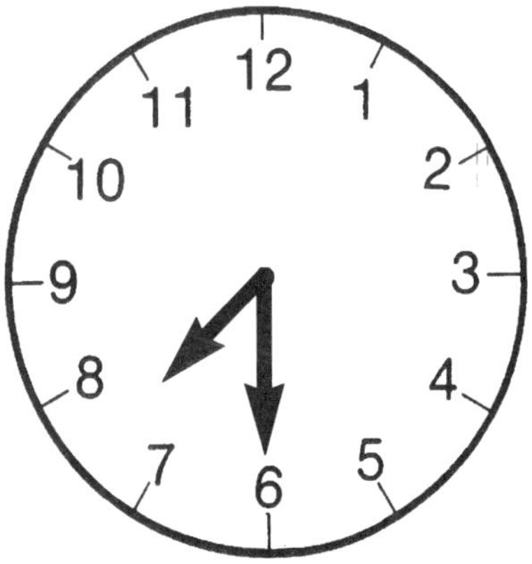

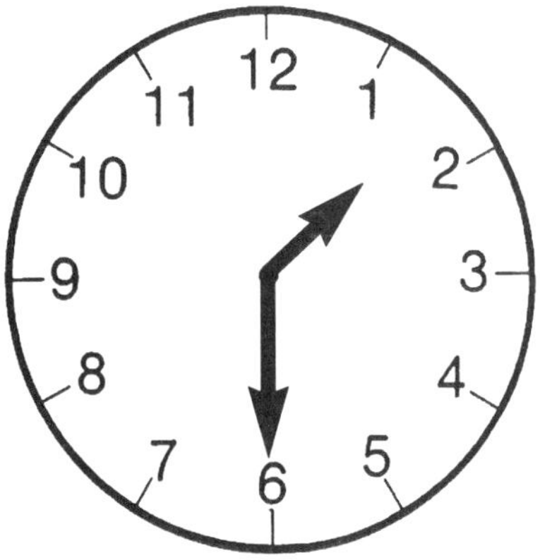

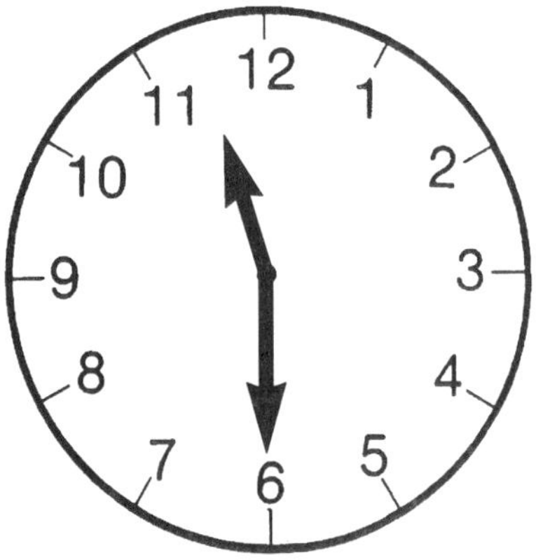

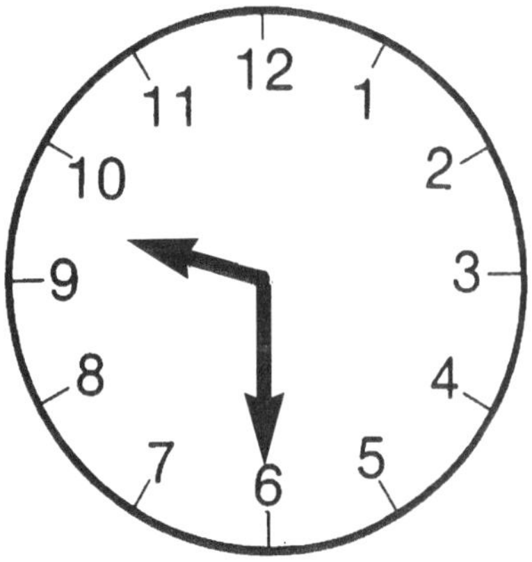

Write the time

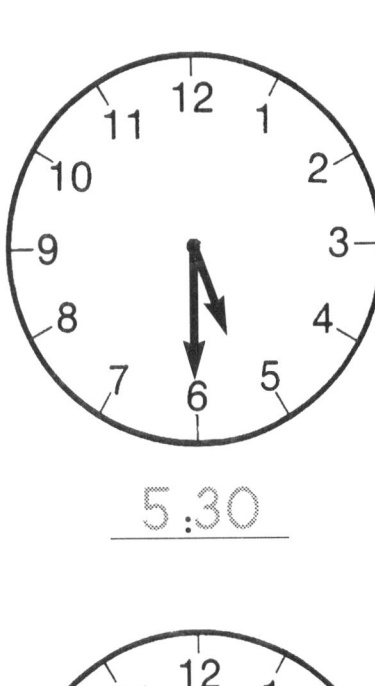
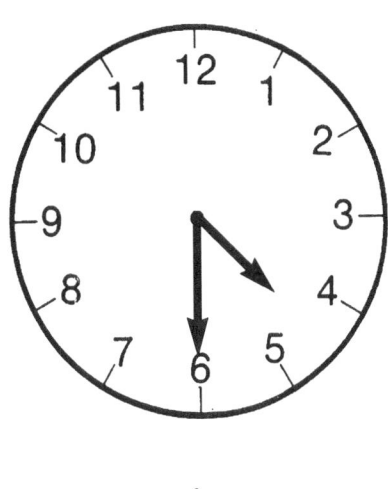
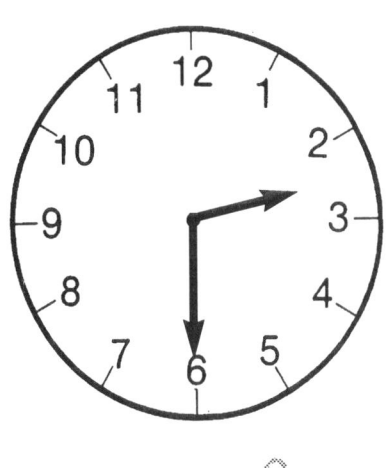

5:30   ___:___   half past 2

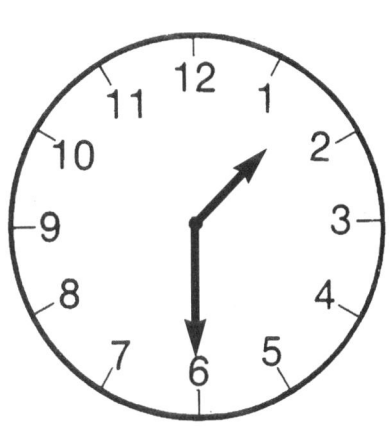
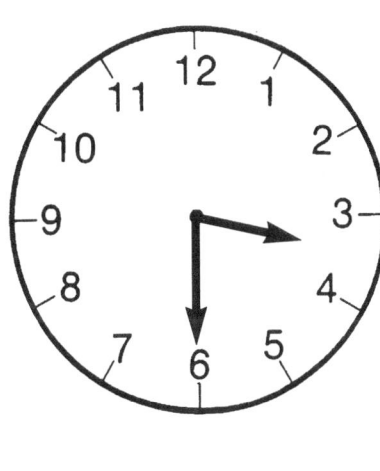
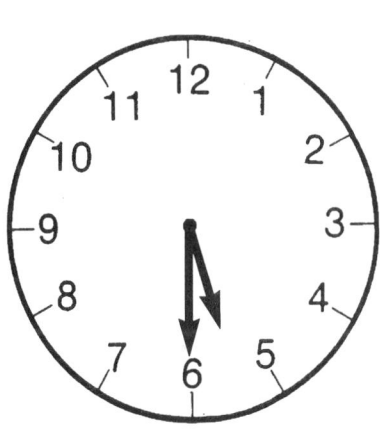

___:___   ___:___   half past ___

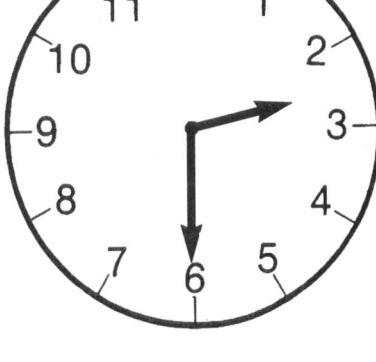
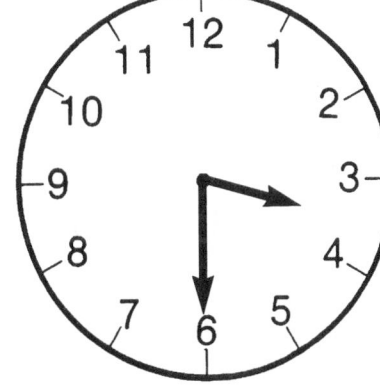
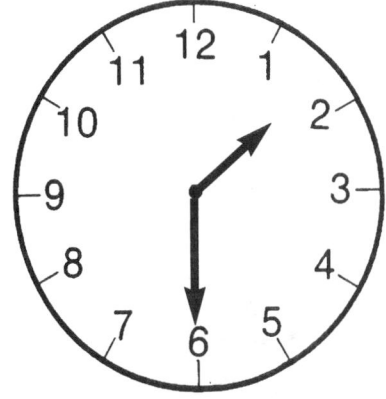

___:___   ___:___   half past ___

Circle the time.

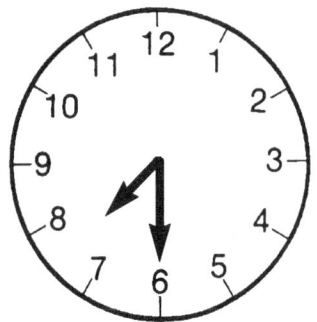

half past 10
half past 6
~~half past 7~~ (circled)

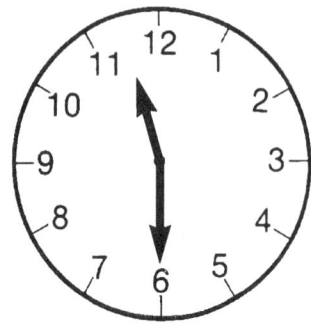

11:00
12:00
11:30

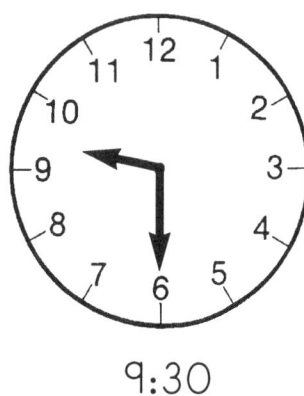

9:30
10:30
6:00

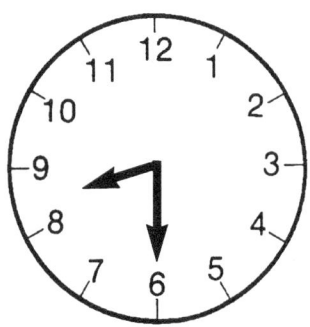

half past 6
half past 8
half past 3

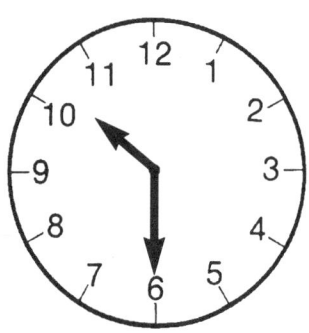

half past 1
half past 10
half past 7

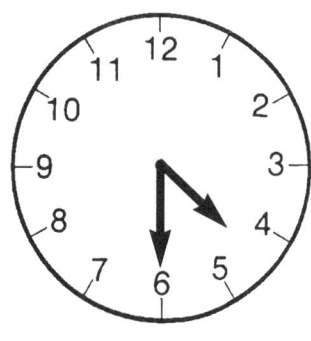

4:30
8:30
1:30

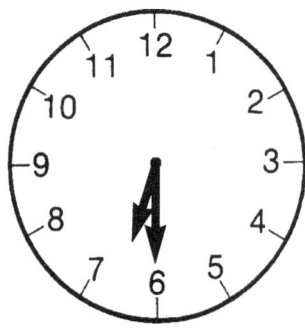

5:30
7:30
6:30

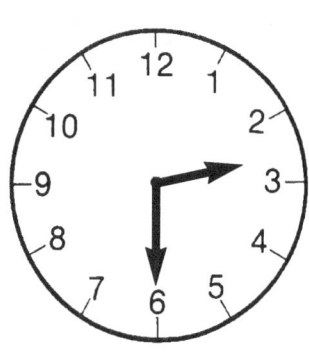

half past 3
half past 6
half past 2

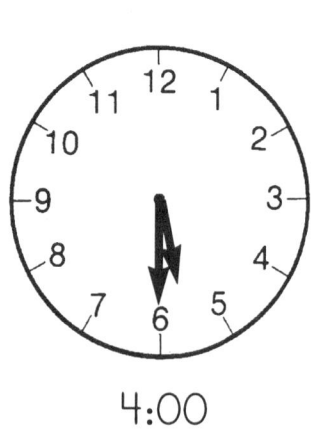

4:00
5:00
5:30

What time is it?

Match.

Write the time.

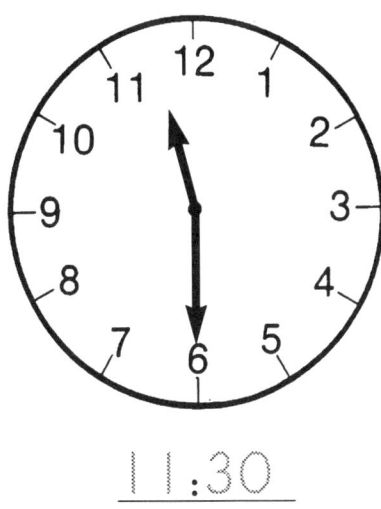
11:30

___ : ___

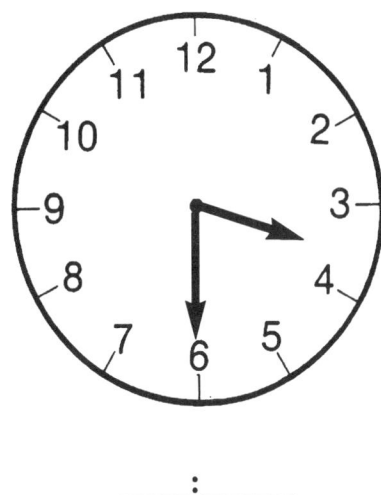
___ : ___

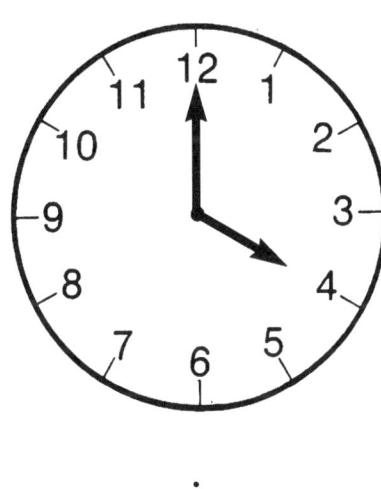
___ : ___

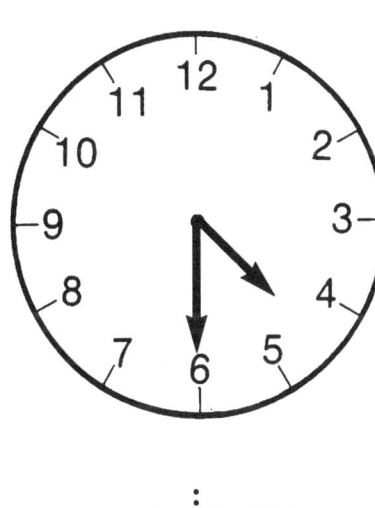
___ : ___

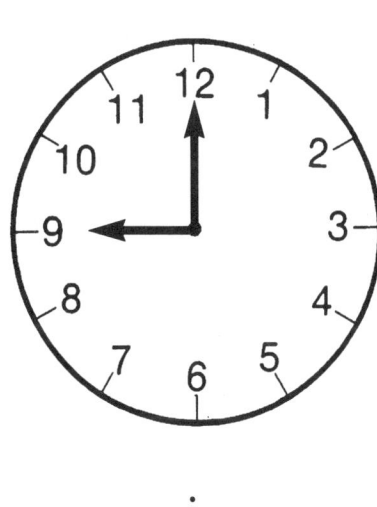
___ : ___

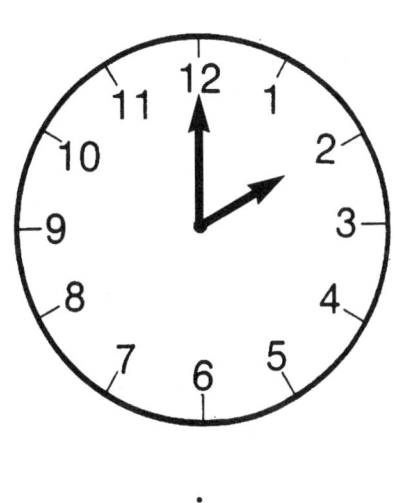
___ : ___

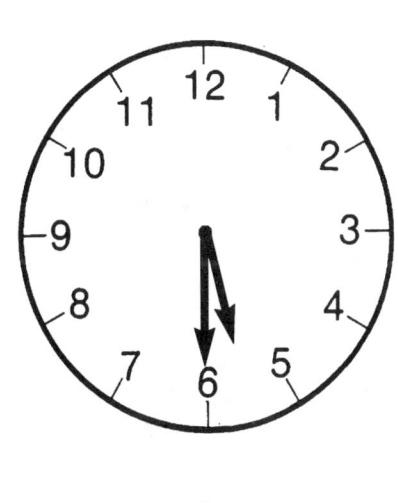
___ : ___

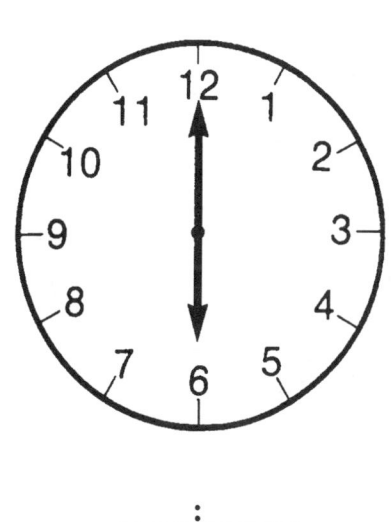
___ : ___

15 Minutes After the Hour

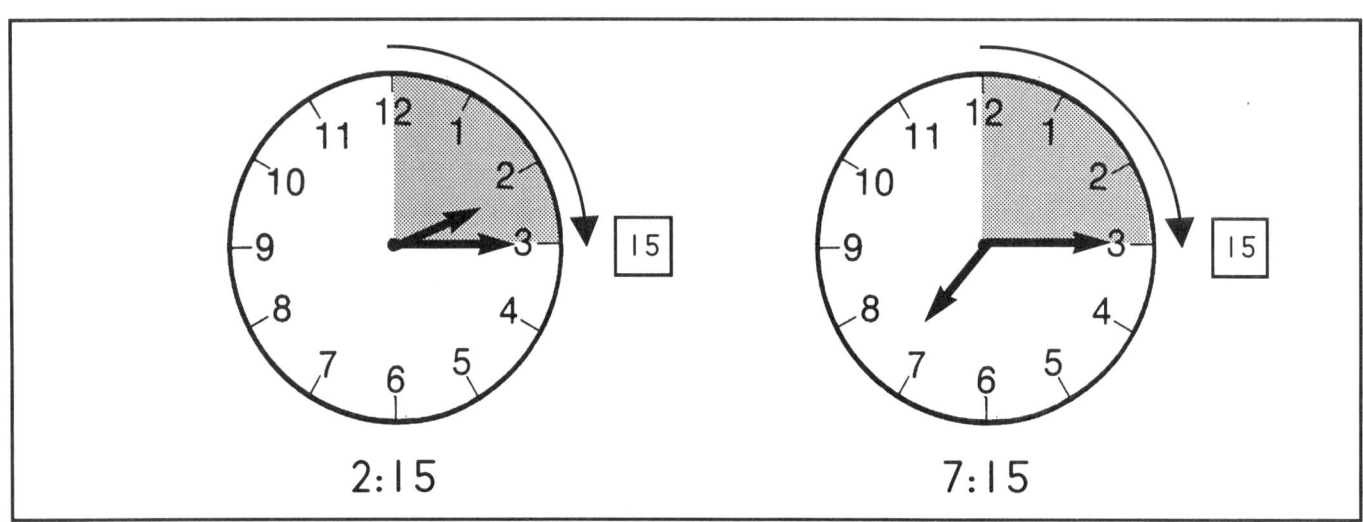

2:15   7:15

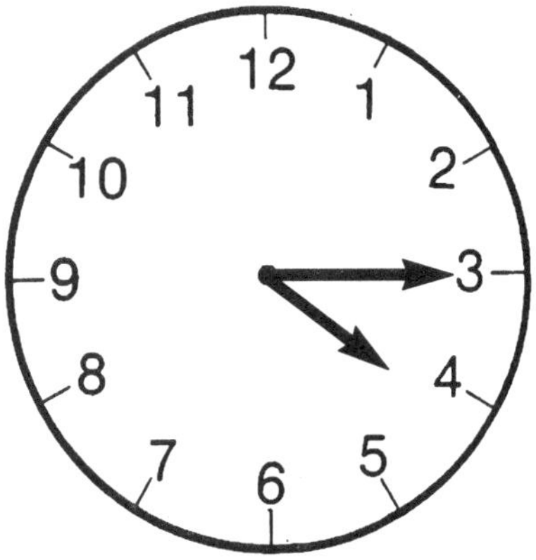

4:15   __:__   __:__

__:__   __:__   __:__

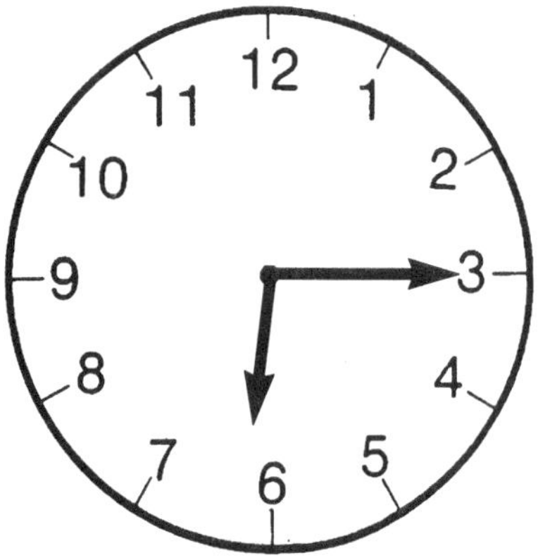

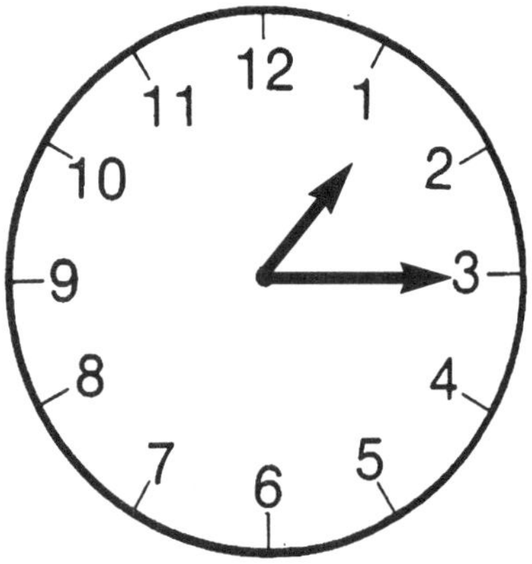

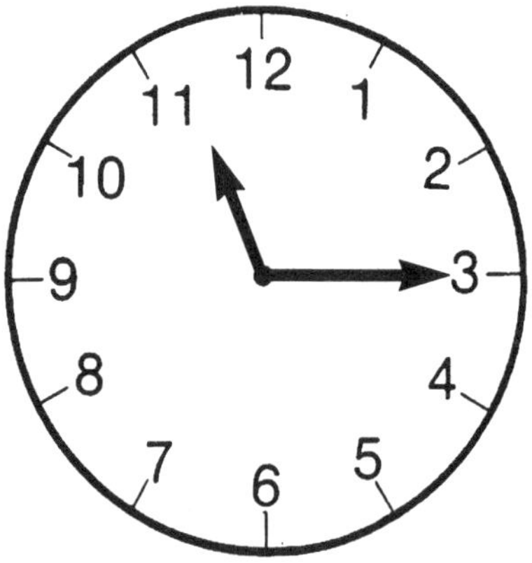

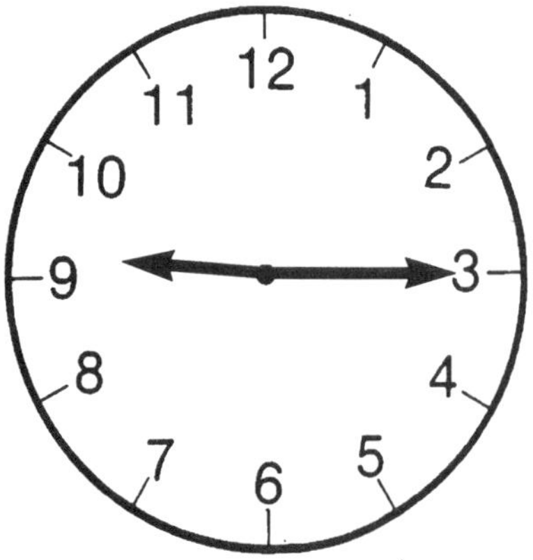

45 Minutes After the Hour

45

2:45

45

7:45

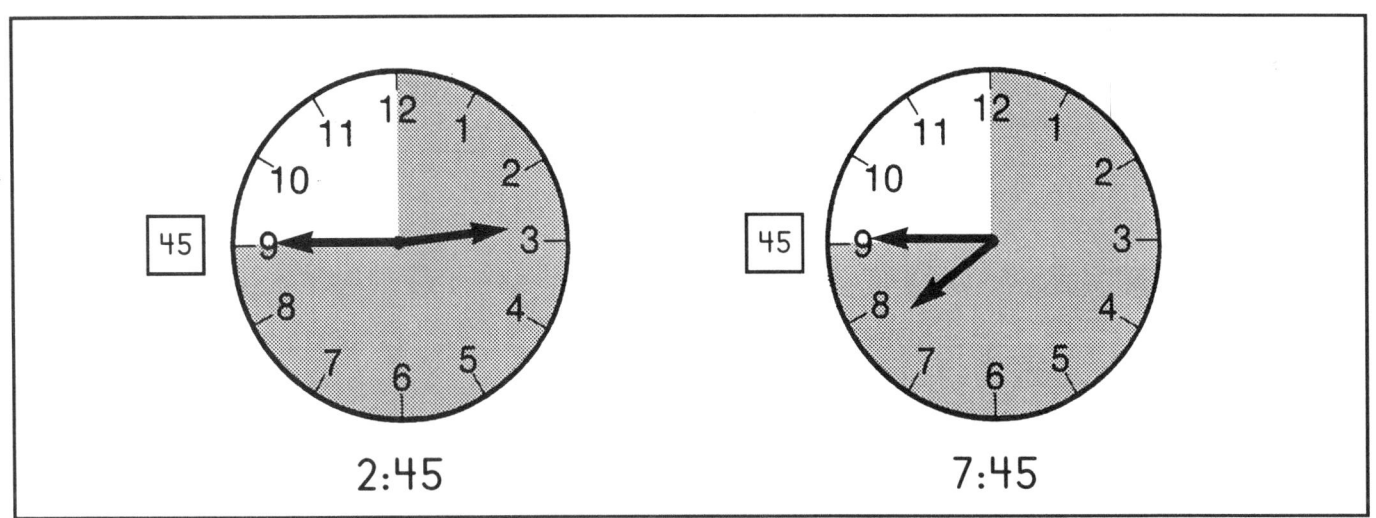

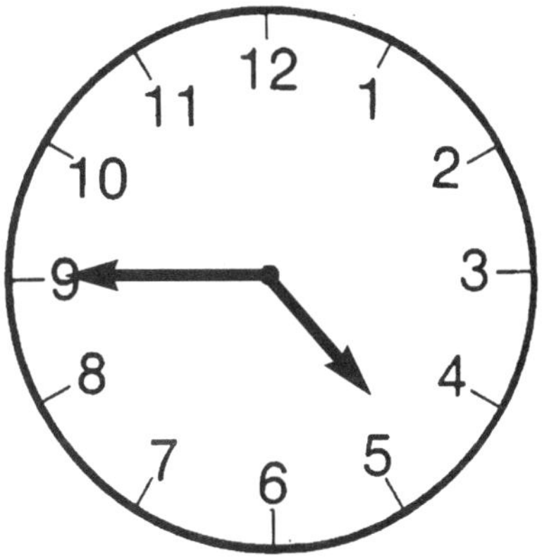

4:45

:

:

:

:

:

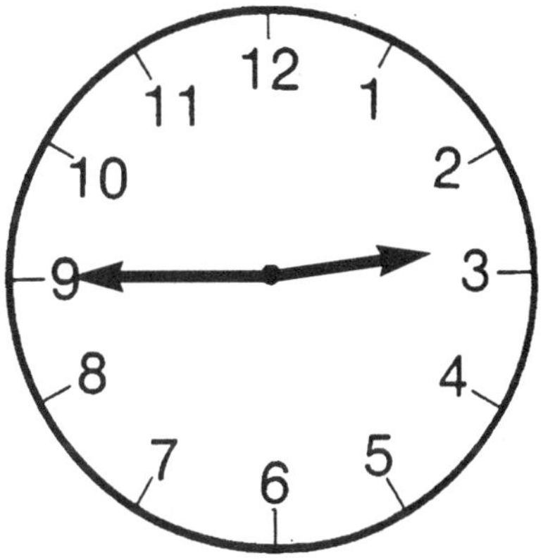

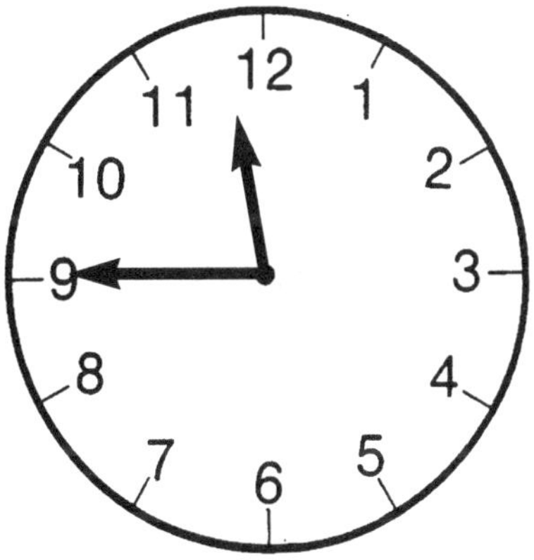

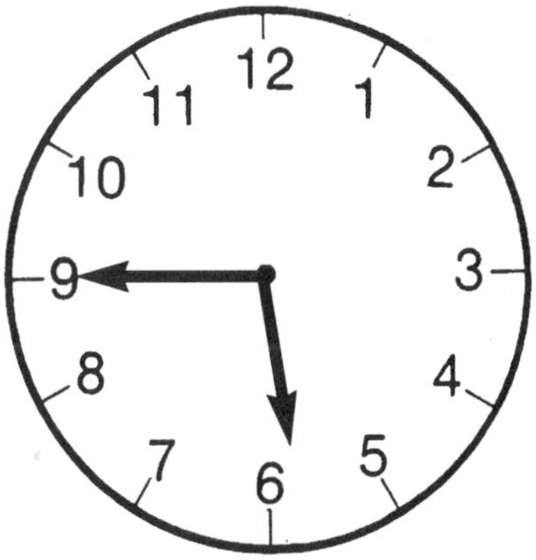

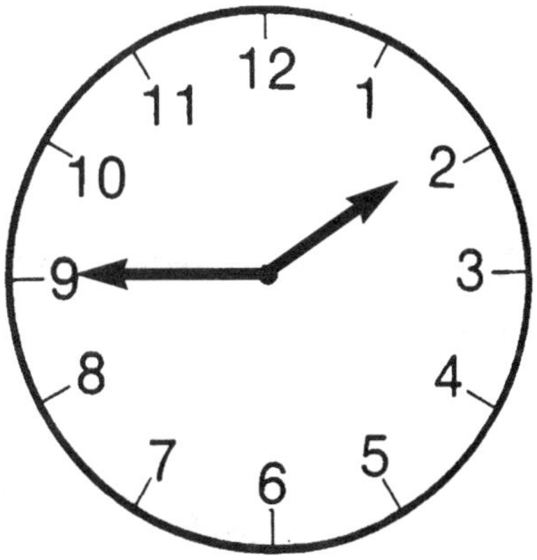

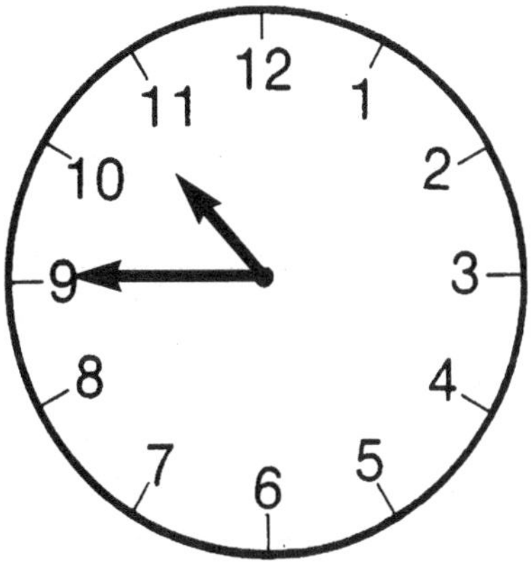

Match.

   3:15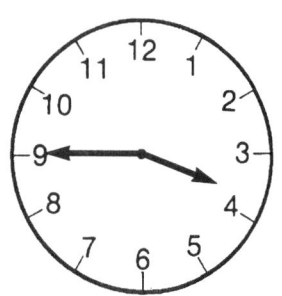
               3:45

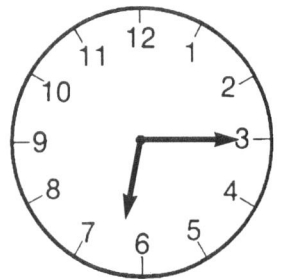   6:45
               6:15

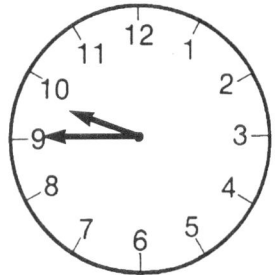   9:45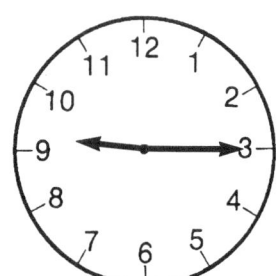
               9:15

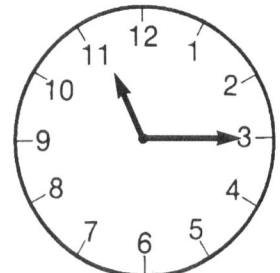   11:45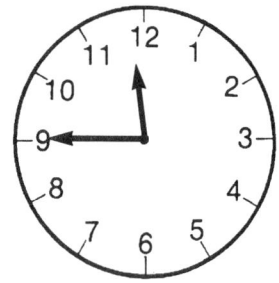
               11:15

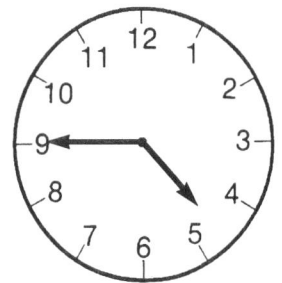   4:15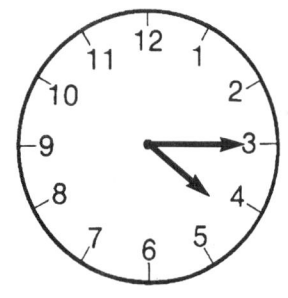
               4:45

Match.

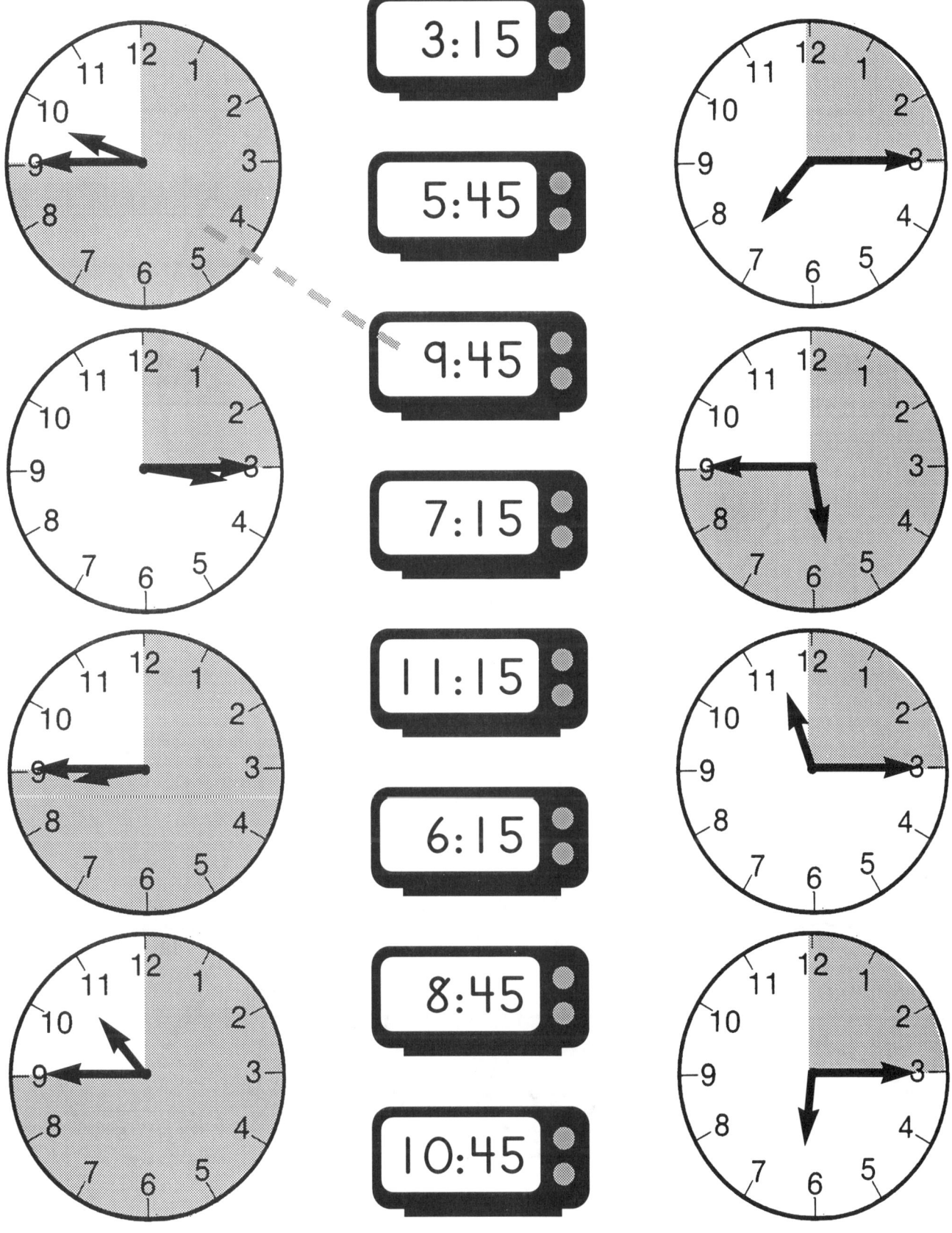

Trace the numbers.

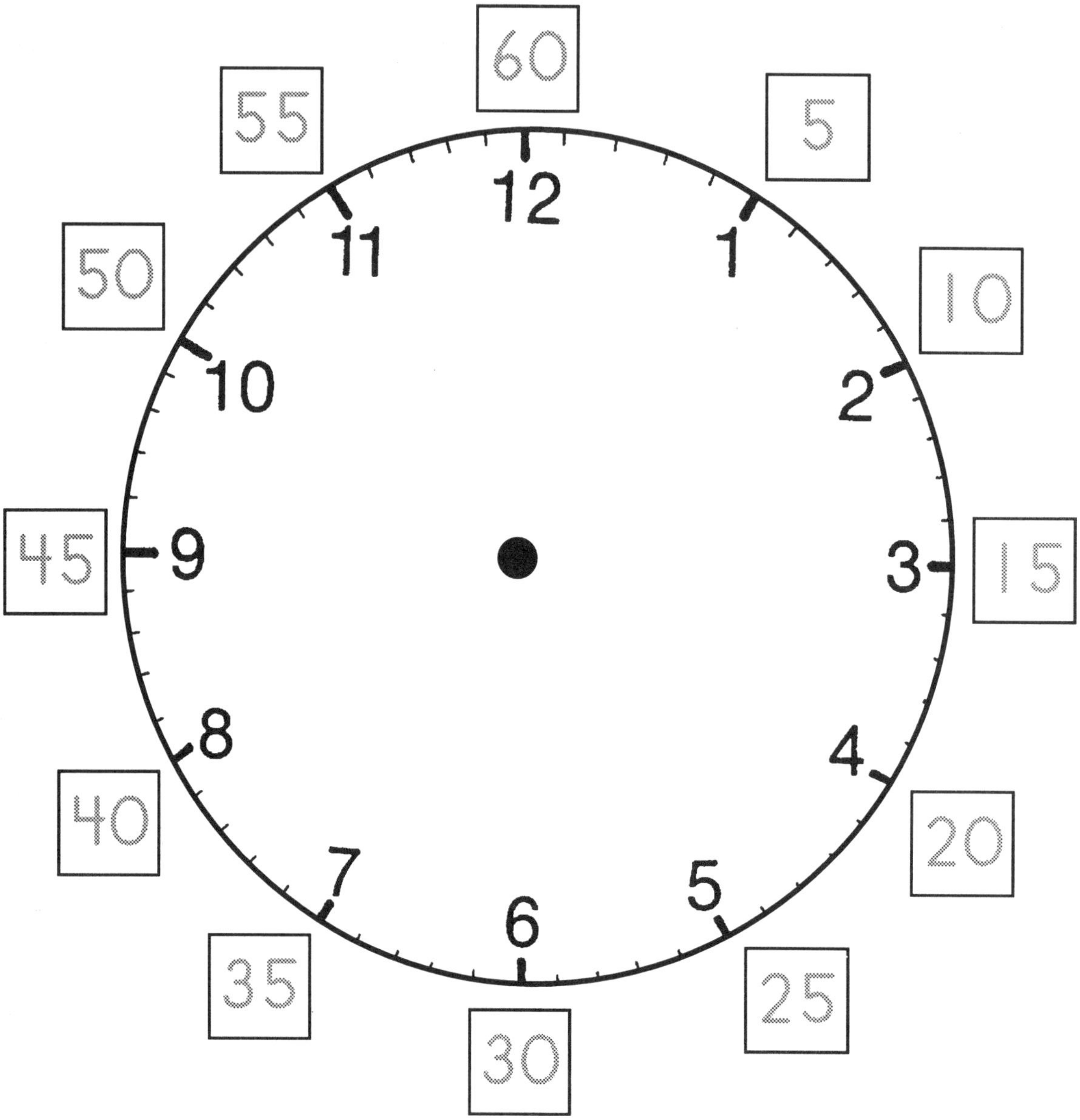

Write.

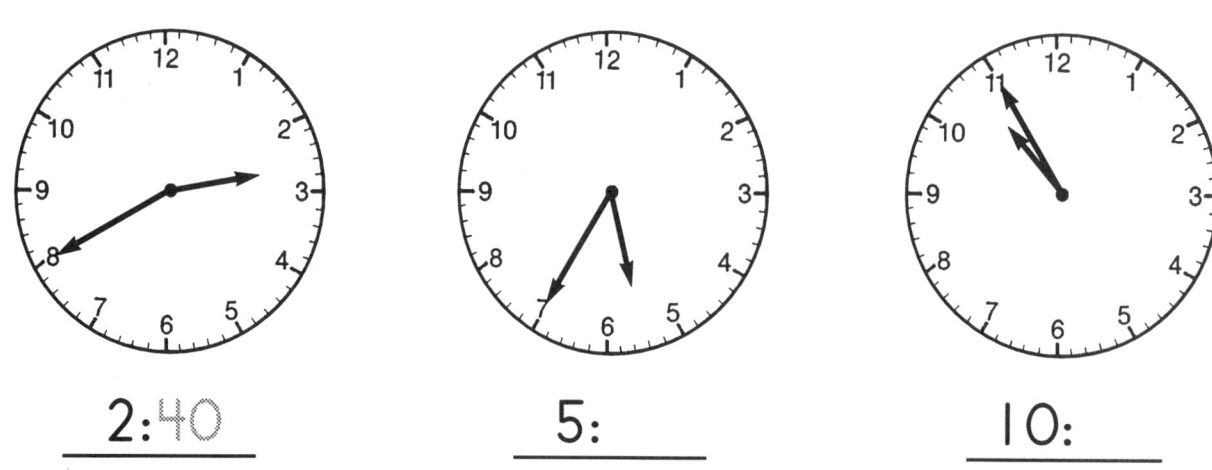

2:40   5:   10:

Circle the correct time.

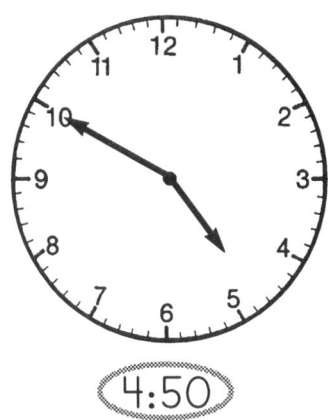

(4:50)
5:10
5:50

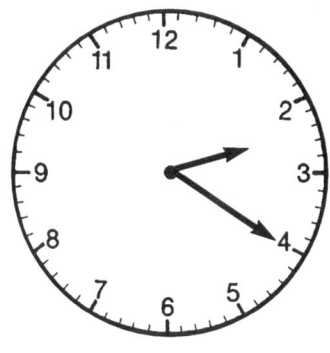

4:10
2:20
1:40

6:40
7:40
8:35

9:35
7:45
8:20

12:55
11:05
11:50

5:05
12:25
1:25

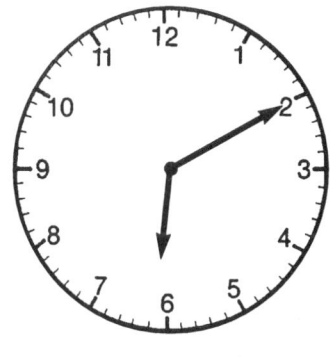

2:30
6:10
1:30

3:55
4:00
11:15

10:15
3:50
9:03

Match.

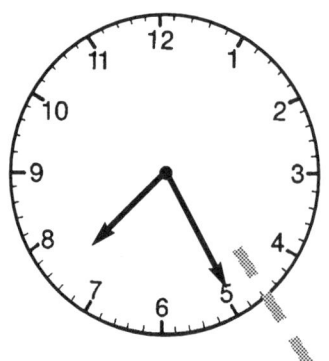

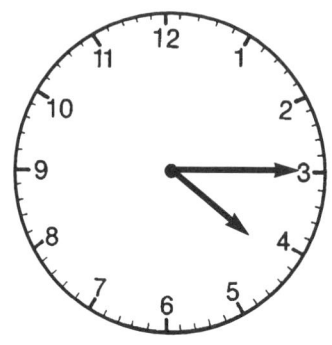

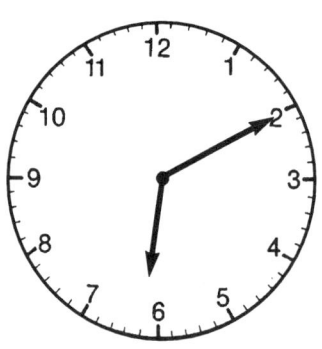

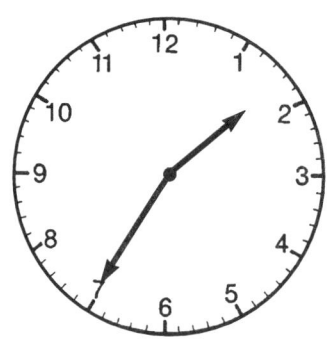

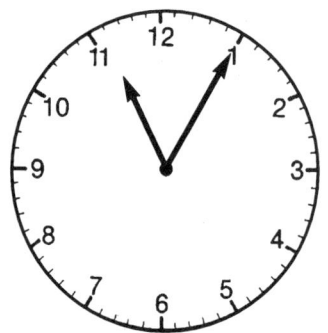

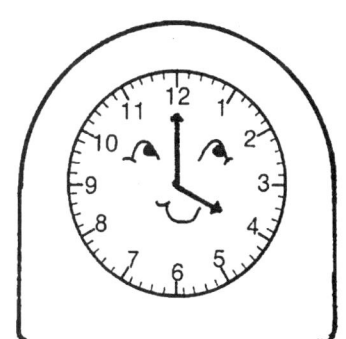

Now—Later

now	1 hour later	now	1 hour later
4:00	5:00	2:10	3:10
8:30	__:__	6:20	__:__
11:15	__:__	9:40	__:__
6:00	__:__	11:05	__:__
9:45	__:__	3:25	__:__
5:15	__:__	7:50	__:__
3:00	__:__	4:35	__:__
7:30	__:__	1:55	__:__

How many minutes?

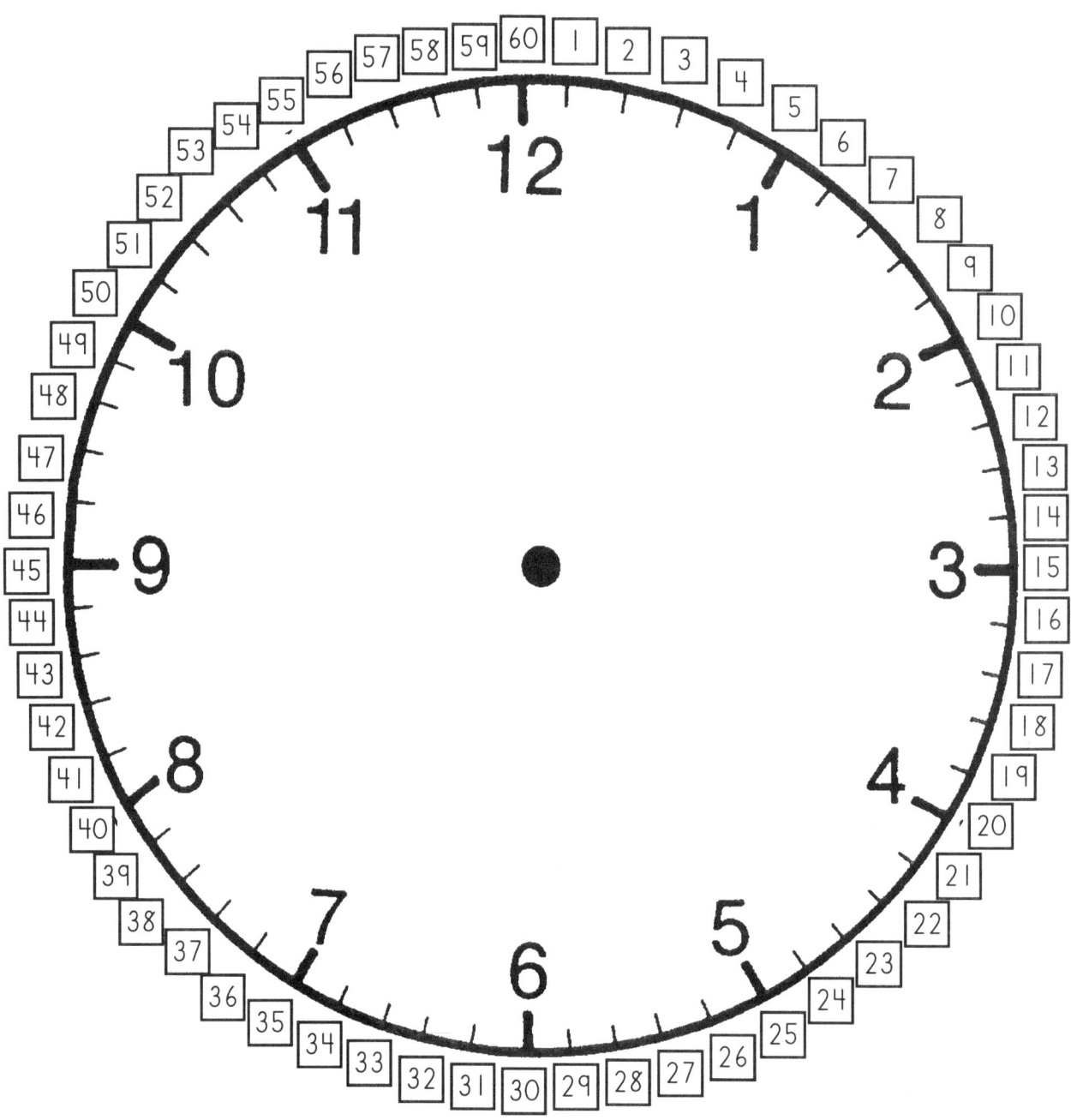

How many minutes are in one hour? ☐

How many minutes are in one half hour? ☐

How many minutes?

Count the minutes.

Match.

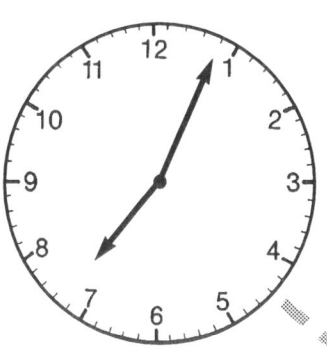

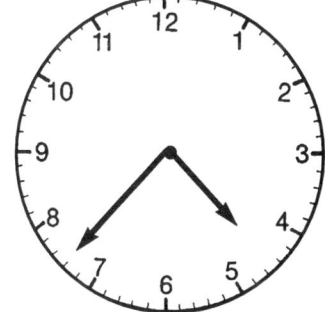

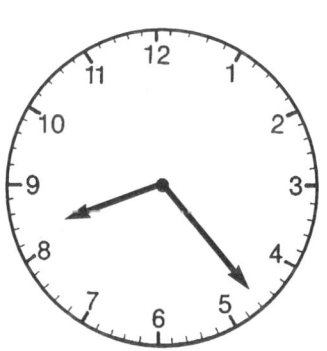

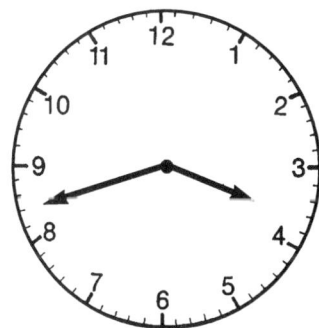

Put the minute hand on the clock face.

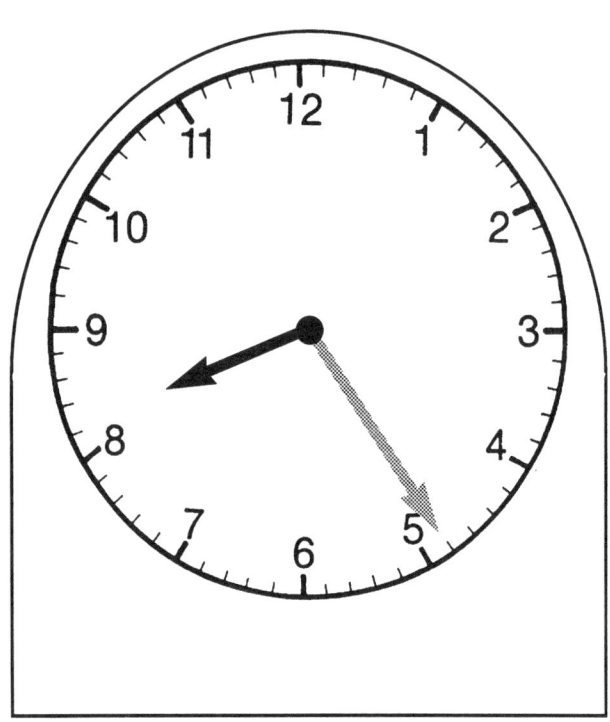

8:24

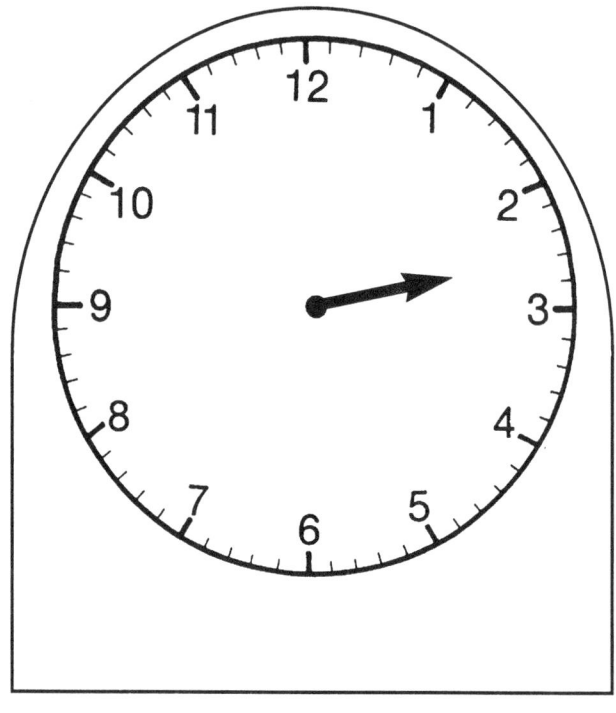

2:26

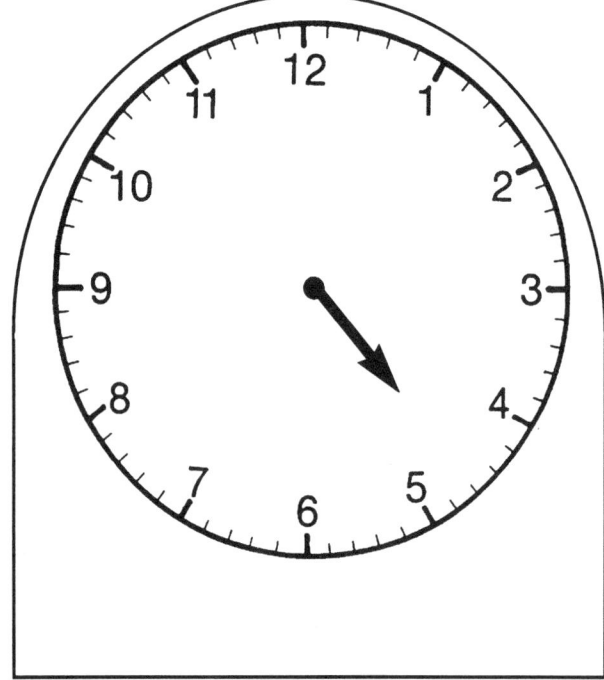

4:38

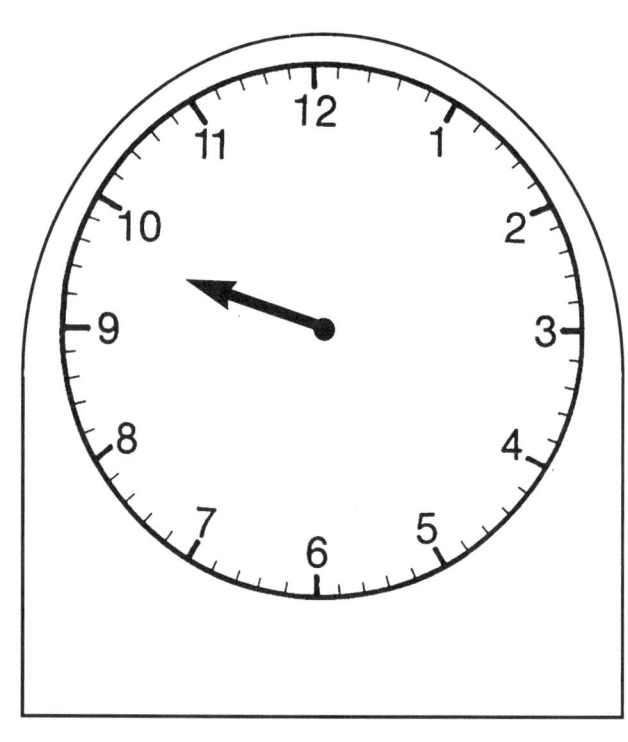

9:40

Put both hands on the clock face.

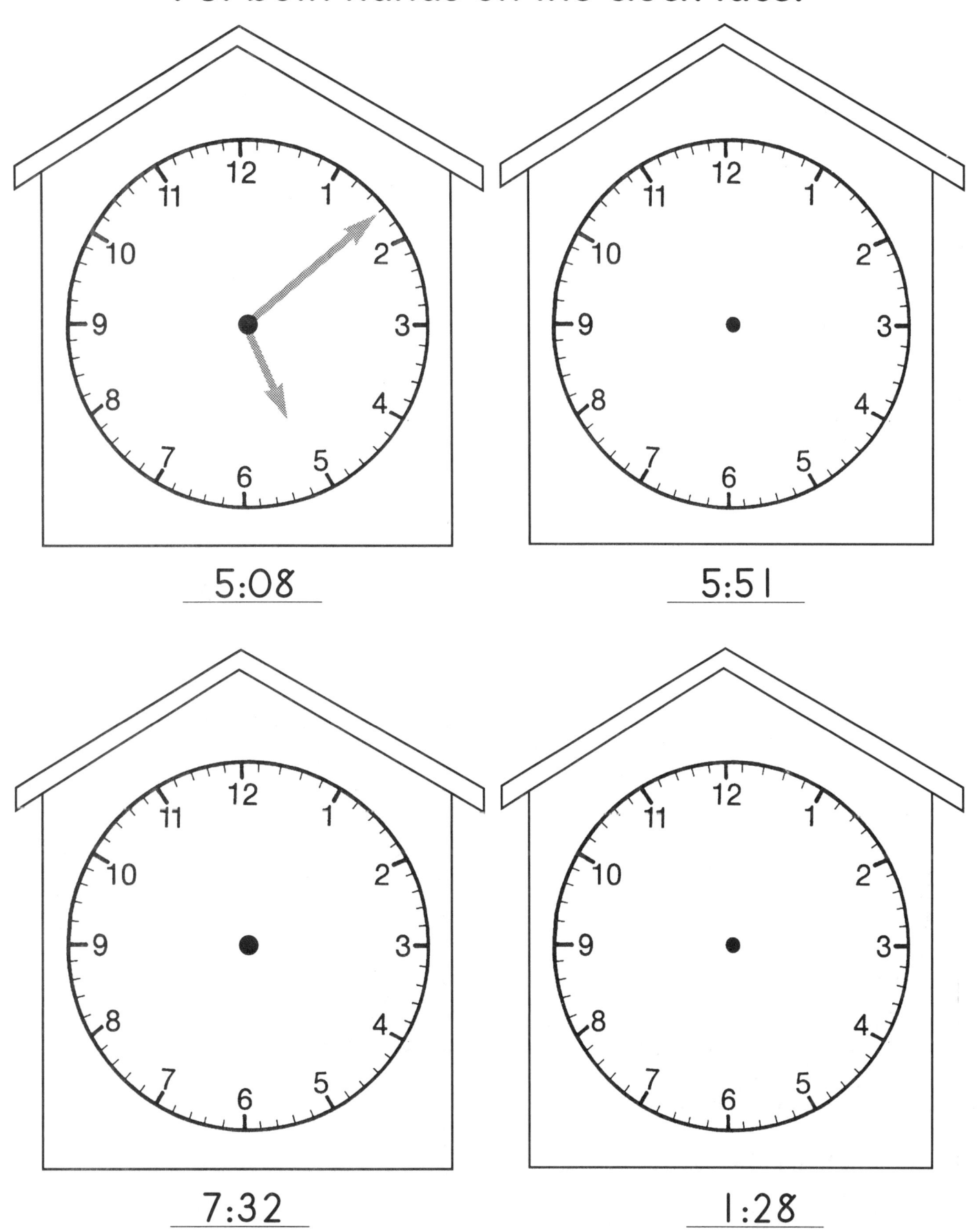

Parents: Help your child keep track of these times for one day.

_____'s Day
your name

Put the hands on the clock.
Write the times.

How many hours did you play? _____

How many hours did you watch T.V.? _____

How many hours did you sleep last night? _____

28

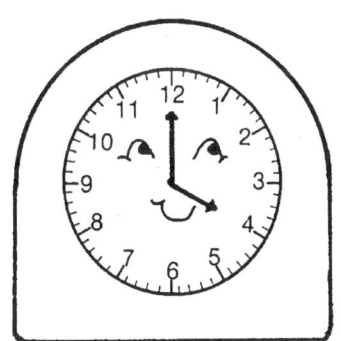

Now—Later

now	in 2 hours	now	in 30 minutes
9:00	11:00	6:30	7:00
6:00	__:__	9:00	__:__
7:30	__:__	2:30	__:__
4:25	__:__	9:30	__:__
11:00	__:__	7:00	__:__
5:30	__:__	11:00	__:__
2:45	__:__	5:30	__:__

Think About Time

1. The soccer game started at 5:30.
   It ended at 7:30
   How many hours did it last?

   _____ hours

2. The show started at 2:00.
   It ended at 4:00.
   How many hours did it last?

   _____ hours

3. The party started at 3:15.
   It lasted 3 hours.
   What time was it over?

   _____ : _____

4. The hike started at 1:00.
   We hiked 2 hours and 15 minutes.
   What time was the hike over?

   _____ : _____

5. I left for school at 8:00.
   I got home at 3:00.
   How long was I gone?

   _____ hours

6. It takes 30 minutes to get from my
   house to the park.
   I left at 1:30.
   What time did I get to the park?

   _____ : _____

Answer Key

Please take time to go over the work your child has completed. Ask your child to explain what he/she has done. Praise both success and effort. If mistakes have been made, explain what the answer should have been and how to find it. Let your child know that mistakes are a part of learning. The time you spend with your child helps let him/her know you feel learning is important.

page 1
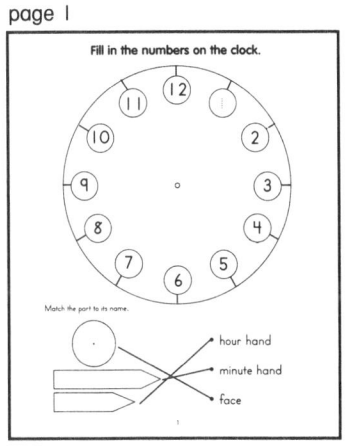

page 2
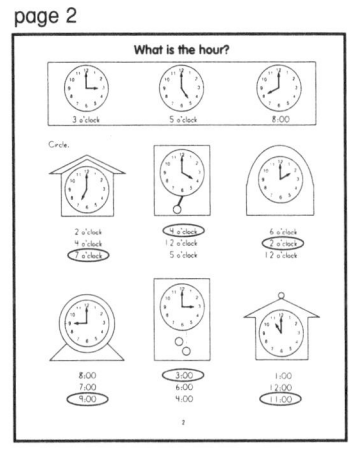

page 3
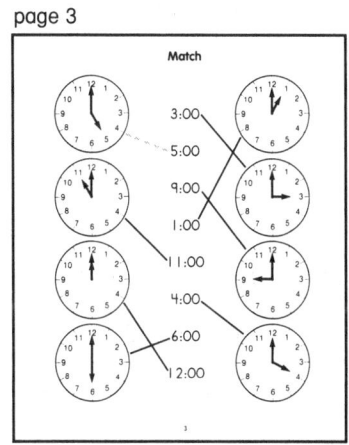

page 4
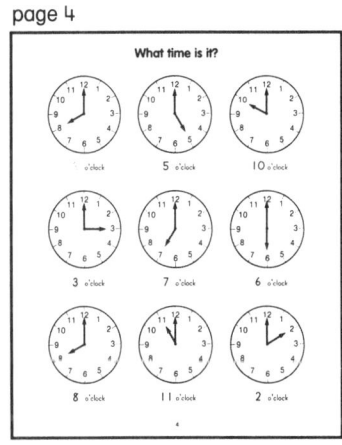

page 5
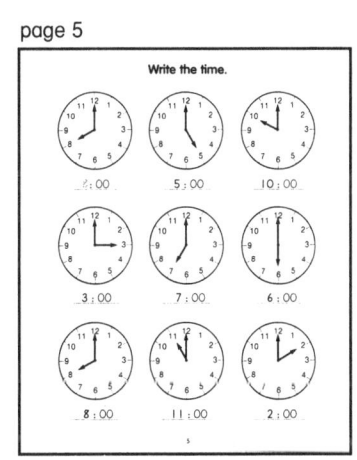

page 6
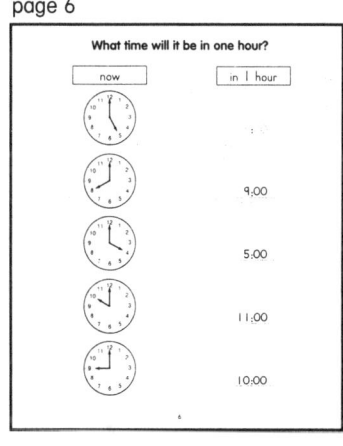

page 7
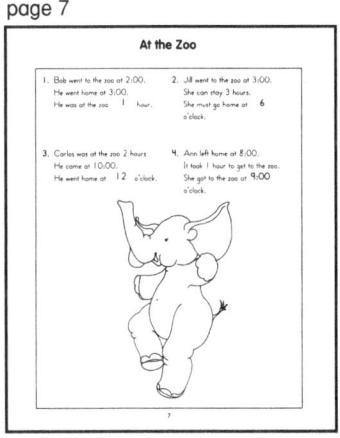

page 8
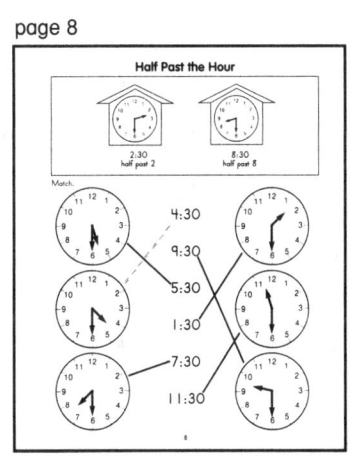

page 9
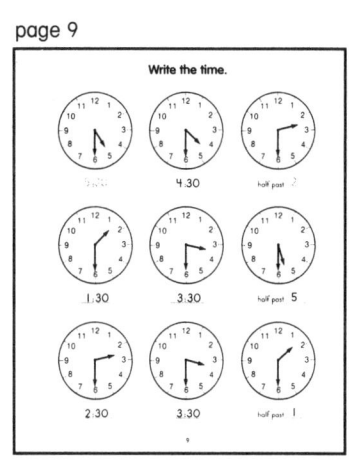

page 10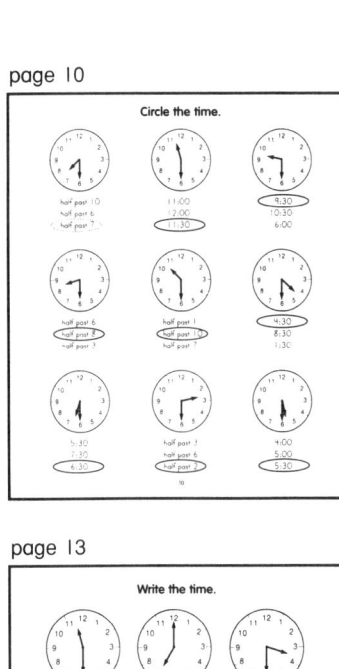
page 13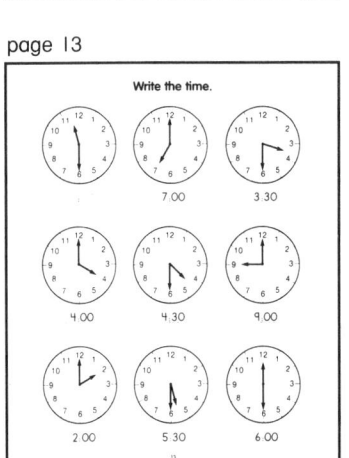
page 16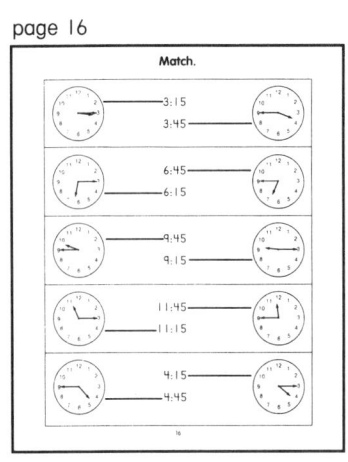
page 19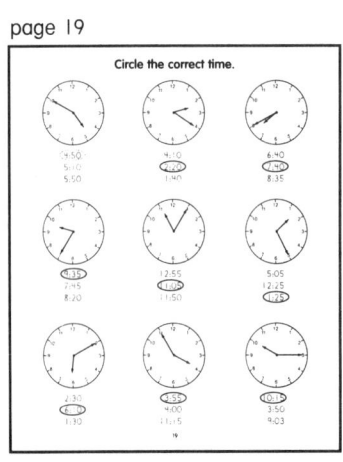
page 11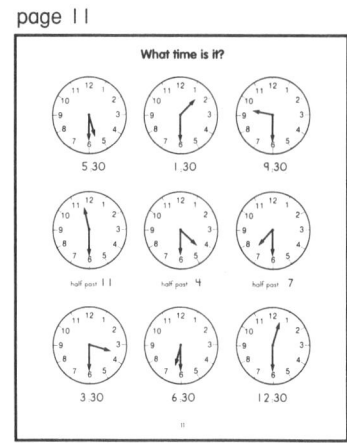
page 14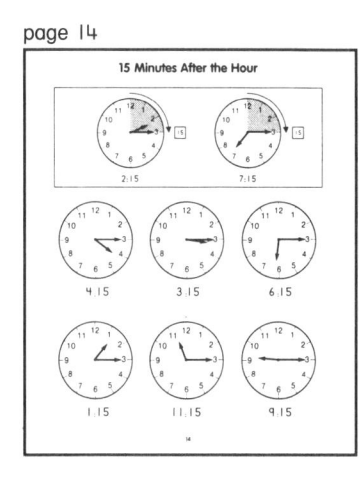
page 17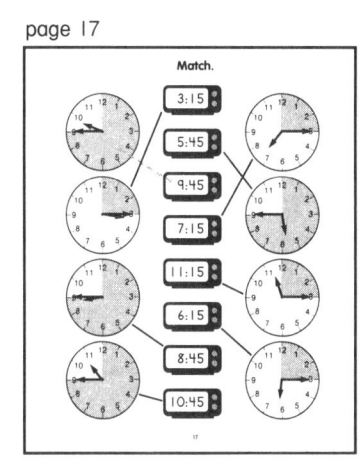
page 20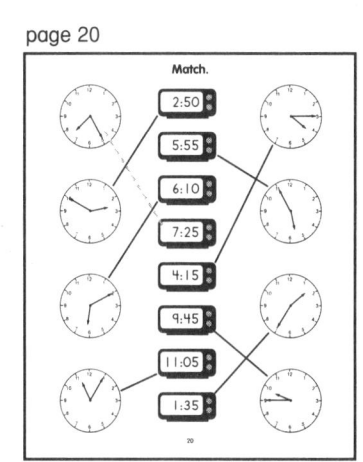
page 12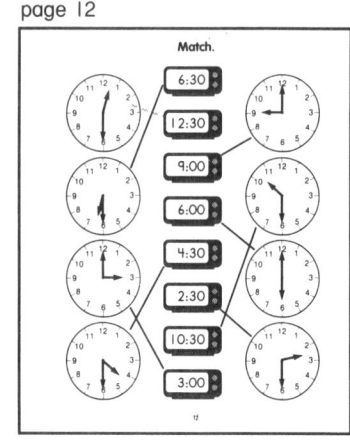
page 15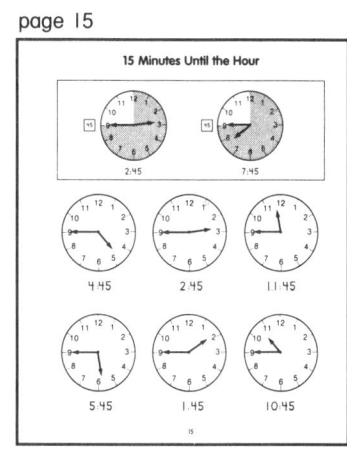
page 18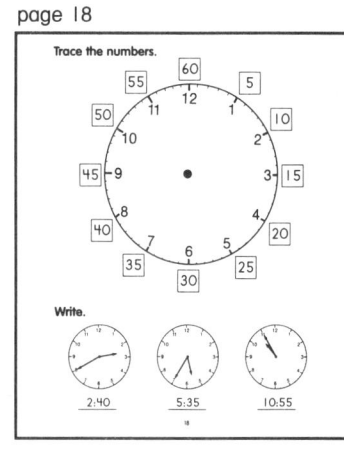
page 21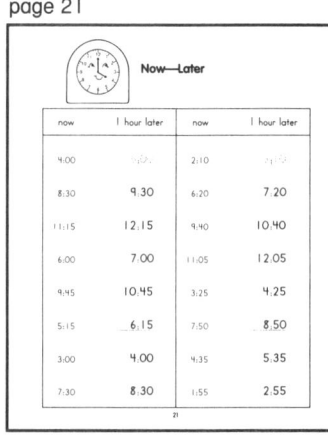